# Secret Genealogy IV
## *Native Americans Hidden in Our Family Trees*

# Suellen Ocean

*Cover Photo is "Plenty Wounds" Indian Male, Library of Congress*

# Secret Genealogy IV
## *Native Americans Hidden in Our Family Trees*
by
### Suellen Ocean

Published by:
Ocean-Hose
P.O. Box 115
Grass Valley, CA 95945
www.oceanhose.com

Also by Suellen Ocean:
*Secret Genealogy*
*Secret Genealogy II*
*Secret Genealogy III*
*The Lies of the Lion*
*The Guild*
*The Last Quadroon*
*The Celtic Prince*
*Gold River*
*Gone North*
*Black Pansy*
*Evaline's Fiddle*
*Acorns and Eat'em*
*The Acorn Mouse*
*Poor Jonny's Cookbook*

# Table of Contents

# *Introduction*

*Umatilla Maiden, Library of Congress*

In August of 1790, a young brother and sister were out in a Kentucky field pulling hemp when six or seven Pottowattomie Indians came running at them from a cornfield. Twelve-year-old Daniel was killed when his skull was crushed by a tomahawk and nine-year-old Sarah was captured and held for five years. After the Battle of Fallen Timbers, Sarah was released and returned to her family and former culture where she later married and lived a long life. Sarah's story is chronicled in the family history. She is remembered by her somewhat eccentric habits acquired when living with the Pottowattomie, including kindling her fires Native style and preferring to live in a wigwam during the summer.

The traits Sarah acquired from the Pottowattomie were not inherited they were acquired. But do you have traits that couldn't have been acquired but must have been inherited? Learning our ancestry helps us to understand our actions, desires, strengths and weaknesses. Our ancestors have shaped our thoughts on spirituality, politics, parenting, and our attitudes about nature.

Speaking for myself, many of the beliefs and customs I use today were acquired during the 1960's when I was growing up in a world where we threw open the doors to *all the cultures*, wanting to know and explore them. I learned about Native American spirituality, Middle Eastern and Asian religious thought and Mexican American culture to name just a few. In college, I gravitated toward classes that taught me about these unfamiliar cultures and today I still enjoy researching cultures different from my own.

I have come to appreciate the inherited traits that live within me, connecting me to ancestors who *recently* lived *with nature*. At times I am confused and want to make apologies for my lifestyle, beliefs and customs that differ from society's norms. I've been fighting this paradox for years. Researching this book has me contemplating nature versus nurture. It is a gift to understand.

My cousins through Facebook saw that I had posted my finished cover of this book while I was still writing it. They volunteered that they remembered their mother (my aunt) saying she was "one-quarter Native American." Why don't people tell you these things? How are they not spelled out, loud and clear? My sister now tells me, "Oh yeah," our mother told her and my brother responds with a "Yup." Why did my mother tell one daughter but only allude to it with me? Her favorite picture of me was always the one where I am on the ground in the forest gathering acorns, it was the first thing I saw when I walked into my parent's home. I was puzzled by her fondness for that one picture. Now I understand.

*The author in 1993 gathering acorns in Mendocino County, California.*

I have included a lot of links throughout this book and know that I could be diverting the reader away from the book but I **strongly** advise you to read the book **first** then go back and use the links.

# *Chapter One*

## *Our Colorful Ancestors*

*Hupa Female Shaman, Library of Congress*

In *Secret Genealogy III*, I promised that *Secret Genealogy IV* would help people find Native American ancestry. Now here I am trying to make good on that promise and I can't even find my own Native American ancestry. It's an extremely difficult endeavor even though there are hundreds of websites and numerous books. The problem for me has always been *too much information*. It is **very** overwhelming. With *Secret Genealogy IV*, I've tried my best to simplify the process and hope the reader finds this book a good starting point to begin their search for their Indian ancestors.

In genealogy, persistence is a virtue. Every day that I worked on this book, I grew to understand Native American history and the politics that surround being "Indian." A year ago, the only thing I had in my family history regarding Native American ancestry was a line my mother gave me about how her family used to sit around the table and think *maybe* they had Indian ancestry because of their high cheekbones. *Maybe?* My mother is no longer with us and she knew that she was indeed of Native American ancestry. When she died, my mother was 92 and the older she got the more Indian she looked. It was weird seeing her like that. She was too old and feeble to go to the beauty parlor, and we let her beautiful thick hair go natural and her thin elderly skin stuck to her bone structure. All I could think was, "Why does my mother look like an Indian?" My older brother finally admitted that my mother's brother, Uncle Harold, told him to "soft pedal that Indian stuff."

As I mentioned above, I have found tracing Native ancestry to be overwhelming. The websites devoted to it are detailed and seem geared toward those who understand the process and probably already know the names, dates and places where their Indian ancestors lived. All I know is that it *might* be on my grandfather's side. But I wouldn't be surprised if I find it on both my mother and father's side. After all, I am a North American. Our earliest American roots date back to 1658. There's bound to be a Native in there somewhere but the problem is... *it was a long time ago.*

My initial reason for writing a book about Native ancestry was to help sort things out and provide a bridge for those seeking clues. All the collective work of genealogists is what's needed. As any good genealogist knows, EVERY CLUE IS IMPORTANT. I'm sorry that information is difficult to come by and that American history and Indian treaties are complex and overwhelming. But the good news is...

*we're guided by the magic, beauty and imagery of our forefathers and mothers and a connection to others who are seeking.*

People are accustomed to respecting scholars with Ivy League degrees. If an author writes for the New York Times, he or she "must" be good. But as laymen and laywomen, we should never underestimate our own power to uncover and write about history. If you have a computer and a lot of time and patience, you too can uncover some magnificent gems.

There are many different Native American cultures. I've heard it said that to compare one tribe to another would be like comparing Italians to Germans. Your Indian ancestors had unique lives and those different ways of life may have you asking, *do I have American Indian heritage in my family?* Only by attending pow wows and traditional ceremonies can one gain a sense of what it means to be traditionally Native American. We can read books and view Native art, but for those of us looking to find Native ancestry we can only speculate. Perhaps the answers are found in the problems that we encounter in our everyday lives, like an inability to fit into the dominant culture. Yet we will never know if our peculiar customs come from our Native ancestors or our European, African, Asian or Middle Eastern ones.

There are customs that you may find in common with Native Americans. One of those customs may be the lack of direct eye contact when meeting someone for the first time. Native Americans may not give you direct eye contact because in their tribe they may see it as rude. Another may be in the handshake. Some Native Americans have a different style of hand shaking. While Europeans may be firm and aggressive with a handshake, Native Americans may have a gentler handshake. They may also have a different concept of time. They may be late to a meeting because they don't live their lives by constantly looking at the clock. In today's dominant American culture, people not only plan their lives in hours, they sometimes plan their lives in fifteen-minute increments in little black books or on their smart phones. Is that difficult to relate to? Do you resent it? Is it hard for you to conform? And Native Americans are often strong with their sense of life as a circle and storytelling is very important to them in their understanding of life and communicating. They may have strong values that are compromised when following the majority's way of doing things and that can cause great distress. Native Americans might not say much but instead, observe by watching. Sound familiar? These differences may have come about through the generations. Although alienation is a common feeling (advertisers prey on it) you may have inherited customs that are a bit different, *they were Native customs.*

When my brother finally admitted that we had Native ancestry, it put into perspective my mother's constant drive to venture into the yard and dig weeds. She loved nothing more than to spend all day digging weeds with a big butcher knife. Now I see that as her "digging stick." As for myself, I love nature and had a strong instinct to gather and eat acorns. I wrote a book about it back in 1993, (*Acorns and Eat'em*). And I loved carrying my baby on my back. Co-incidence or lingering inherited traits?

7

There are more than 550 tribes in the United States. They lived in this land we call America, they cared for it better than we care for it today. If European exploration had not occurred, Natives may still be living much the same way they lived for thousands of years. But the lost tribes are gone now (and there were plenty of lost tribes) and we can't bring them back and if the Europeans had not explored, most of us would not exist. Funny how life is.

Because America was and is such a melting pot, many of us haven't a clue what ethnicity our ancestors were. Terms like Northern European don't quite cut it for me, although I remember in my pre-genealogy days, I was so desperate for anything, I was thrilled when someone told me my ancestors were definitely Northern European because of the way I looked. I've since learned I'm a classic example of America's melting pot. I've become quite a collector of ethnicities.

While doing the research for this book I was confused. All the lists of Indians were mostly Cherokee. I found myself looking for the other tribes when I should have realized they died in Indian wars. But still... I kept asking myself, *where are they?* The answer is, they live within us, which is why we have this insatiable drive to esoterically touch our finger to theirs, to at least feel that we know they were here and though the name of their tribe and the words that spoke their names are lost, they are not forgotten.

In the 1800s, a Cherokee Indian named Sequoyah created a syllabary of the Cherokee language and the tribe built a printing press and published a newspaper, the *Cherokee Phoenix*. Unfortunately, the military destroyed it but it did not stop the Cherokee people. If there ever were survivors, it's the Cherokee. If you don't believe me, get on the Cherokee forum on the genealogical websites where they're very good at speaking their thoughts and sharing their knowledge.

If your family is from Oklahoma, Arizona or California, it may help to know that those three states have the highest number of Native American residents. Next is New Mexico, North Carolina, Washington, Texas and believe it or not, New York, in that order. Except that for many of us, our Native ancestors were not originally from those areas but were *removed* from their homelands and relocated to new territories.

*Quote*

Today, many Lenni Lenape live on the reservations in Oklahoma. Throughout these centuries, however, some remained in Pennsylvania, intermarrying and assimilating into the dominant culture. These ancestors hid their Native heritage to protect their children from persecution, and at times, death. In Native culture, decisions are made with the future generations in mind. Only in the last few decades has it been possible for the descendants of those ancestors to begin to practice their religion and culture again. It is a tribute to their ancestors and their efforts to ensure the future survival that today many say, "There are no Indians here in the East." In truth, there are thousands of them, and they have begun to reclaim their heritage.

http://www.anthro4n6.net/lenape/

There were almost three million people living in the United States who stated on the 2000 census that their race was either American Indian or Alaska Native. Forty-three percent of these Natives made their homes in the West, thirty-one percent in the South, seventeen percent in the Midwest and nine percent in the Northeast. Think of the millions of people who wouldn't think to list their ethnicity as Native American but have a little of the blood running through their veins. If our grandparents didn't tell us they had Indian ancestry, we certainly aren't going to check that box.

Because it's difficult to prove Native American ancestry, most of us will have to be content with our family oral history and looking at the pictures of our ancestors. On the genealogical boards there's occasional bickering about who's Native American and who isn't. I'd ignore that. Everyone wants to be proud of their heritage. If all we have is a piece of oral history, then so be it. Yet, even though it's fair to footnote our family records as "oral history" and legends are *wonderful*, at the end of the day, what's important is *truth*.

When researching for this book, one of the other researchers said that he would use "American Indian" to specify one who was a card-carrying member of one of the five-civilized tribes and "Native American" to refer to all the rest. I use the words Native, Native American, American Indian and Indian. I use them all and think of them as synonymous... but I'm quite sure there is controversy over the different terms and their definitions.

Don't rule out French-Canadian history in your family tree, there is no ocean between Canada and America, immigration went back and forth. Hundreds of years ago, French explorers began traveling through the rugged country of New France, followed by trappers and traders. Marrying a Native woman empowered a man because Native women knew the language, were hearty in the cold wet climates of the north and they could translate. They made excellent assets in their husband's business affairs. And we mustn't neglect to mention that women make wonderful mothers and delightful companions, although I am a bit biased.

The "Scots-Irish", were a lively group who came to the early American colonies with the hope of a better future. By the time they got here, in large numbers, Scotland and England had been fighting terribly. The Scots who lived along the border with England became very good warriors. When the Scots-Irish came to North America, they were accustomed to fighting with the English so probably gave Native Americans a difficult if not impossible time. But Native Americans and Scots-Irish frequently intermarried. Scots-Irish surnames are abundant on Native American lists of names. There are also Jewish surnames on that list. (For more information on hidden Jewish ancestry, see my previous books in this series, *Secret Genealogy I, II & III.*)

Although there are scores of tribal names, most of the Native American tribal names translate to mean something like, "we the people," or "people of the river," that sort of naming pattern. But when

Europeans came to Native lands, they often referred to tribes by the derogatory names called them by rival tribes. For this reason, many Navajo prefer to be called Dineh and I heard a Native speaker on the radio one day say that Apache was not the name of their tribe but a name the cowboys used. Nor is Eskimo (Inuit and Yupik are more appropriate) and the Sioux are the Dakotas (Lakotas). Sioux is a shortened version of a derogatory name given them by their enemies. The list of culturally incorrect tribal names is quite long and unfortunately the names persist and I use them when applicable to tell the history. And of course, most of us know that the name "Indian" arose through Christopher Columbus, believing he had found his route to India, although that has become controversial. Some believe that Columbus's name for the Natives was actually a Spanish expression *in Dios,* meaning *with God.*

*Quote*

The tribes are generally known by names given them by white people. This is one of the most singular facts in history... Indian tribes have within themselves several names, just as individual Indians have frequently half a dozen names; some have signed treaties with several names.

REPORT ON INDIANS TAXED AND INDIANS NOT TAXED IN THE UNITED STATES (EXCEPT ALASKA), **ELEVENTH CENSUS 1890**

We are all "mixed breeds" of one ethnicity or another. Half-breed was a common expression in the past and the old definition of Mestizo.

Mestizo derives from the Latin word *mixtus*, which means mixed, which is what we all are, no matter what color our skin. Mestizo was used historically in reference to someone who had one parent who was Spanish or Portuguese and the other who was American Indian. A Mestizo may also have been of Jewish ancestry because many Jews escaping the Inquisitions of Spain and Portugal went to the Americas and were silent about their ethnicity, presenting themselves as Spanish or Portuguese. When these Spanish or Portuguese Jews intermarried with Native Americans and had children, their children were labeled Mestizo. It's similar on the Canadian side and areas of American states bordering Canada where the word is "Metis", for the descendants of the French and Native intermarriages. Metis also refers to the descendants of African American intermarriages with French Canadians as well.

Because the Irish and Scots Irish intermarried with Native Americans and African Americans, Metis becomes a very multi-ethnic expression. If one started in Canada and traced down the Mississippi River into Louisiana, then Texas and down into Mexico, the word is Mestizo the farther south you get and Metis is used up north.

Many Native American tribes were (and are) very creative. They love storytelling. Through their stories we hear the history of our ancestors. They also loved leisure activities like playing games. They loved to sing and taught their children through their songs. Maybe these are attributes your parents inherited from a long-lost culture, because for those of us looking to uncover any clues to Native ancestry, it's buried very deeply.

*Quote*

... Native Americans soon recognized that the Europeans themselves were very human. Indeed, early records show that 16th- and 17th-century Native Americans very often regarded Europeans as rather despicable specimens. While Europeans, for instance, were frequently accused of being stingy with their wealth and avaricious in their insatiable desire for beaver furs and deer hides. Likewise, Native Americans were surprised at European intolerance for Native religious beliefs, sexual and marital arrangements, eating habits, and other customs. At the same time, Native Americans became perplexed when Europeans built permanent structures of wood and stone, thus precluding movement. Even village- and town-dwelling Native Americans were used to relocating when local game, fish, and especially firewood gave out.

**Sandra L. Cadwalader**

http://autocww2.colorado.edu/~toldy2/E64ContentFiles/HistoryOfThe Americas/NativeAmericans.htm

# Chapter Two
# *Where Do We Start?*

*A Paviotso Indian of Pyramid Lake, Library of Congress*

Where do we start? I cannot stress it enough. Start with TEAM WORK. Get on the genealogical/ancestry message boards, put the time in and make use of the hard work done by other researchers. Familiarity is IMPORTANT. We are spying on these people, though they are no longer with us, we want to know their story.

If a descendant of a brother of one of your ancestors is posting on a genealogy forum about his ancestor and that he was half Choctaw and there is no mention of your g-g-g-grandfather, you'd probably skip right past the posting, especially when there are 500 other posts. But if you're FAMILIAR with your ancestors and their families, you'll catch it. Same thing about geographical locales. If you read the message posts enough, and study your ancestors and the messages other relatives leave on the message boards, you'll see mentions again and again of the states, counties, parishes, cities, towns, etc. where they lived. Be ready to catch those clues, all it takes is one to open up their world.

Get all oral history from living relatives. Search ancestry.com, genealogy.com and any other genealogical sites. It isn't just Native American ancestry sites where people discuss Native ancestry. On the major genealogical sites participants talk about their ancestors being "Indian" frequently.

If money is not a factor for you, subscribe to ancestry.com. But if you don't wish to subscribe, you can still use their services. You can set up pages at no cost and start uploading your family tree. You can also read ancestry.com and genealogy.com's extensive message boards. From their main page, look for words like "community" or "collaborate." You can search for surnames, states, groups, etc. Here's a good topic rundown:
Message Boards > Topics > Ethnic / Race > Native American > Nations >Cherokee >

Learn to use the ancestry message boards to your advantage. There is no end to the search words you can use. Try searching through the entire site as well as just the surname forums. If they have an ethnic group like, "Black Dutch" (Natives often used that ethnicity to hide) or "Cherokee" go through all those that could apply. Odd names may work in your favor, common names are difficult but not impossible. It's trial and error and the process of elimination.

Genealogy.com has no message boards for Native American, American Indian or Indian. Not even for Cherokee. But ancestry.com does. From their main page go to collaborate, then to message boards and topics. You'll find discussions and it's free to read them. A lot of the talk is about ancestors "captured by the Indians." There are hundreds of stories. Once you're in the topic you can at least plug your surname in the search field and see if anything comes up.

*Quote*

In the early part of this century, there were many reasons for leaving your Native ancestry unclaimed. In those days a "guardian" was assigned to full-blooded Native Americans to manage their affairs. Many times the "guardian" benefited more than the Indian did. Voting was a privilege denied Native Americans and women until 1924. Women were discouraged from registering by their Anglo husbands, especially if they were living outside the Indian Territory. Probably the most fearful reason was the removal of the Native Americans to Oklahoma Territory. The reasons varied, yet all had merit to the Native American at that time in history.

**State of Alabama, Indian Affairs Commission**
http://www.aiac.alabama.gov/Gen_cherokee.aspx

Unless you have something to go on, how would you know where to begin? First, you have to have a generation or era in your tree that you believe holds a Native ancestor. Then you have to narrow it down and work feverishly to prove it. But how? First begin with an ancestor's name. Do a google search with their name and the word "Indian" next to it. Or, if you're researching the name Loretta Chartier you can search for "Native American Chartier" or "Indian Chartier." "Indian" was used in the past and I see it all the time but with the realization that Indians were from India, Native American or American Indian is commonly used. With my family, we speak of our "Indian" ancestry, understanding we don't mean, from India. Go through the Google entries and learn everything you can. If someone is discussing that Loretta Chartier was Indian, it will come up.

I've been lucky with my genealogical pursuits but my success usually comes from persistence and trying variations. I rarely rule anything out. I get leads and I build on them. I can't tell by an ancestor's name whether they were European, African American or Native American. The names John Spencer and James Albert sound English. They do not give red flags that this person was a slave but they are authentic names of slaves freed through the Underground Railroad.

I spend years reading blogs and ancestry message boards. I never give up. It took me thirty years to find anything about my husband's matriarchal line because his grandmother was so proud of being the granddaughter of a Churchill, she used that surname, though it wasn't even her maiden name. There's a famous columnist with exactly the same name. Every column she wrote for years was in the Google feed making it impossible to read about anyone else with the same name, but every chance I got, I kept trying variations of names and finally I ran across an obituary for her brother. Now I've got my husband's ancestry coming out my ears.

If you know the community in which your ancestors were born, do a Google search of the community and study everything you can about that community's Native American history. Dig deep into the search engine. What you're looking for is probably on page seventeen of the search engine. Every time you search you'll probably feel exhausted afterwards, I do. But after you shut your computer down, ideas will emerge. You'll wish you hadn't been so hasty and dismissed that woman's posting on the message board or been close-minded to someone's idea that the name was spelled incorrectly. It feels like the ancestors are guiding us. Believe in the impossible.

Don't be afraid to ask people on the message boards to help you. The worst that can happen is that they say no, or you receive no response because no one knows the answer.

This is an ancestry thread, something you can do later, after you finish this book. Enter your surname and see if it comes up:
http://boards.ancestry.com/topics.ethnic.natam.nations.cherokee.chero kee/mb.ashx?o=600&to=2509&dc=50&dir=forward

I suggest you take what information you have and start a timeline. Title it by the main surname but in parentheses put other surnames as they arise. Arrange the timeline by year. Fill in the timeline with important dates from history like the Revolutionary War, the Civil War, Indian Wars and Indian removal dates. If your ancestor is from Lacine, Kansas, google Lacine and find out its history. Ah ha! Lacine is French for "City of the Swan." If the community has a French name it may have been settled by French immigrants. Not always, but it's a strong clue. Finding that your ancestor was French could lead you back to French Canadian and then to the Metis indigenous culture. Research everything you can about the town, the county and the history of the state or territory during the time of your ancestors.

Try compiling all your research into a timeline by date, like this:

## <u>Lindsey - Morris Timeline</u>

1792 - (about) Bery Morris is born in KY. He is the father of William L. Morris.

1798 - (about) Lytha (D'Lytha?) Morris is born in Kentucky. Lytha is the mother of William L. Morris.

1800 - Early 1800's (or before) Robert Lindsey Sr. is born in Virginia. Robert Lindsey Sr. married Mary Reynolds. Their son is Robert Lindsey Jr. [Could Mary Reynolds be the Indentured Servant?]

1810 - (about) Calvin Hanly was born in Tennessee. Calvin is the father of Martha J Hanly. (It may have been O'hanly originally.)

1813 - Ann E Hanly was born in Tennessee. Ann is the mother of Martha J Hanly.

1819 - Robert Lindsey's Jr.'s wife, **Martha V. Wright** is born in Ohio. Her father and mother were born in Pennsylvania.

One of the most important things you can do is study pictures of both Native Americans and Native Canadians (Metis). Get to know what the face, bone structure, eyes and nose look like and compare them with your ancestor's pictures if you have them. After a while, if not right away, you'll develop a sense for the physical appearance of those who inhabited the North American Continent for thousands of years. If your ancestors were Native Americans, it will come through. Then spend time looking in the mirror at yourself. Any resemblance? Even slight?

We don't need to assume there was intermarrying between *ancient* explorers who came from different countries, including Europe, Asia and the Middle East, we know there was. Through the ages, peoples of the world have paired up, giving us diverse genetic makeup which DNA testing reveals.

*Quote*
"The presence of Vikings in the New World has been proven archaeologically at L'Anse aux Meadows, Newfoundland, and backed up by considerable historical evidence from Norse documents. But many other early Atlantic and Pacific crossings and transoceanic connections have been proposed. It has been shown that even before boats were generally seaworthy, small wooden or reed craft could complete ocean crossings. Thor Heyerdahl's modern-day *Kon-Tiki* and

*Ra* crossings demonstrate at least such a possibility. With the extensive sea travel made over the centuries for fishing and trading purposes in more rugged vessels, plus the strong westward ocean current in the South Atlantic and eastward current in the North Pacific, it seems probable that some unintentional drift voyages did occur. It also seems likely that other pre-Renaissance sailors besides the Vikings were curious about what lay over the oceans."

Carl Waldman, **Atlas of The North American Indian**, pg 82

If you've read my other Secret Genealogy books, you'll know my writing is about *mixtures* of people. There are a lot of politics and arguing when it comes to the subject of Native People. Because of those politics and governmental policies, many of our ancestors hid their origins. Yes, there was genocide toward Native People, which is why these ancestors are hidden in our family trees.

Wars decimated much of the Indian populations. They had to fight against the Dutch, the Spanish, the French, the Russians, the Catholic Church, the Protestant Church and Christianity in general. To remove the Natives from their lands the Europeans went to war with them. Eventually, the Natives wound up quite a distance from their homelands. As Carl Waldman says in *Atlas of the North American Indian*, "Pioneers claimed the land; politicians instituted policies to remove the Indian obstacle from the land; merchants, bankers, speculators, and other business tycoons invested in it, and soldiers patrolled it."

If we have nothing but a hunch, before we can begin we need a story, even if it's a foggy one. Start with a setting (geographical locality) like Illinois that your family is from. Find out what tribes were in Illinois. You can do that by going to: http://www.Native-languages.org/states.htm, where you'll find a map of the United States. By clicking on states, you'll find the tribes. Clicking on Illinois teaches us that there were seven "original" tribes. The Chickasaw, Dakota Sioux, Ho-Chunk (Winnebago), Illinois (Illini), Miami and Shawnee tribes.

We learn that there were seven more tribes that migrated into Illinois after the European population explosion. They were the Delaware, Kickapoo, Ottawa, Potawatomi, Sac and Fox and the Wyandot tribes. Believe it or not, today there are no federally recognized tribes in Illinois.

Now what in the world can we do with this information? Nothing now, just keep the list. The map website has a link to a list of Native American place names in Illinois where you may be able to make a connection to your ancestor's home and that of a tribe. The website also has a link to a Native American encyclopedia. If you're anything like me, you are looking for some quick answers. I don't believe you're in luck there. Sit back, relax and admit that you now have a new pastime, studying Native American history, because it is within that history where you will find the clues you need. At the very least, you'll learn what your ancestors went through and a little of what it feels like to be "Indian."

Next we need a list of Native American names to look at. Maybe we'll find our great granny's name on it. Googling "Illinois Native American surnames" brings up websites, including www.censusfinder.com/indian-census.htm. This link leads me to an ancestry.com website where I'm able to type "Illinois" into the *select a state* search field. It brings up a list of Illinois census records. You have to scroll past the trap that ancestry.com has set for you to go through their site. You'll become familiar with avoiding that. If there is an offering of a census list that's highlighted or a different color, that's where they are steering you to join their paid site.

The search for Illinois Native American surnames has brought me to: CENSUS OF KASKASKIA, 1787. Because I do lots of genealogy I recognize Kaskaskia as French Canadian. In this census the names are mostly French and this would be valuable to those seeking "Metis" ancestry.

There are interesting message boards at *cyndi's list* where they discuss Native ancestry but there's a lot of spam mixed in with the serious discussions. http://www.cyndislist.com/Native-american/queries/

This free website, http://www.accessgenealogy.com/Native/illinois-indian-tribes.htm, will also give you more Illinois history and the option to search for other states.

It is known that many Africans intermarried with Native Americans. Less widely known is the fact that many Native Americans also owned African slaves, and fathered children with African slave women. In addition, there were smaller numbers of Free People of Color who lived in many of the nations and who also lived and married persons from the same nations, and whose descendants claim ancestry from the Oklahoma Black Indian people. As a result, thousands of Americans have African and Indian ancestry.

http://www.Nativeweb.org/resources/genealogy_tracing_roots_/

I am surprised how many states are named after the Indian name for those territories. Twenty-seven out of fifty are taken from Native languages.

+Alabama - Choctaw Indian words alba "plants, weeds" and amo "to cut, trim or gather"

+Alaska - may be a corruption of the Aleut Indian word for "great land" or "that which the sea breaks against"

+Arizona - comes from an Indian word meaning "few springs"

+Arkansas - the name of an Indian tribe

California - may be Spanish and mean "hot furnace"

Colorado - comes from the Spanish word for "red"

+Connecticut - Indian word meaning "long river"

Delaware - named after Governor De La Warr (Virginia's governor)

Florida - Spanish meaning "feast of flowers"

Georgia - named after the English King George II

+Hawaii - from the Native Hawaiian word for "homeland"

+Idaho - comes from Indian words, means "light on the mountains"

+Illinois - Indian word meaning "the river of men"

+Indiana - named after Indians

+Iowa - named after a Sioux Indian tribe means "sleepy ones"

+Kansas - the name of a Sioux Indian tribe, may mean, "raven"

+Kentucky - Iroquois Indian means "land of tomorrow" or "dark and bloody ground"

Louisiana - named after the French King Louis XIV

Maine - named after an ancient French province

Maryland - named after English Queen Henrietta Marie

+Massachusetts - Algonquian Indian meaning "big hill small place"

+Michigan - Indian word meaning "big lake"

+Minnesota - from the Sioux Indian word meaning "sky blue water"

+Mississippi - from two Indian words maesi "fish" and sipu "river"

+Missouri - named after a Sioux Indian tribe

Montana - Spanish and means "mountainous"

+Nebraska - Indian word meaning "wide river"

Nevada - Spanish word meaning "snow clad"

New Hampshire - named after Hampshire England

New Jersey - named after the Channel Island of Jersey

+New Mexico - Mexico is an Aztec word for their national god

New York - named after the English Duke of York

No & So Carolina - named after English King Charles I or French King Charles IV

+No & So Dakota - Dakota Indian word meaning "alliance of friends"

+Ohio - Iroquois word meaning "great"

+Oklahoma - Choctaw Indian word for "red people"

Oregon - from the French word ouragan meaning "hurricane"

Pennsylvania - named after William Penn

Puerto Rico - Spanish for "rich port"

Rhode Island - named after its resemblance to the Mediterranean island of Rhodes

+Tennessee - comes from an Indian word meaning "curved spoon"

+Texas - Indian word meaning "friends" or "allies"

+Utah - named after the Indian tribe "Utes"

Vermont - French words verd "green" and mont "mountain"

Virginia & W Virginia - named after Queen Elizabeth the "Virgin Queen"

Washington - named after George Washington

+Wisconsin - an Indian name

+Wyoming - Algonquian Indian meaning mountains and valleys alternating. (Algonquian pertains to the most extensive of the linguistic families of North American Indians. These include: Abnaki, Arapaho, Blackfoot, Cree, Delaware, Micmac, Ojibway, Massachuset Sac and Shawnee.)

The following maps are but three of the sixty-seven maps of Indian "land cessions." (Cession means to give way, a yielding as of property or rights, to another.) They were compiled by Charles C. Royce for a report made to the Smithsonian Institution in 1896-97. These "cessions" came about through treaties or "other legislative mechanisms." These maps are helpful when trying to understand the migration patterns and regions where your ancestors lived. They are not crowded with Interstate highways and an abundance of cities and towns. I strongly urge you to take a look at them, it will help you to understand the territories and make evaluations on where your ancestors may have gone. There are treaties that go with these maps, 375 of them are housed at Oklahoma State University. The University of Nebraska in Lincoln has another nine.

To view all sixty-seven maps go to: US GenWeb Archives, United States Digital Map Library, http://usgwarchives.net/maps/cessions/

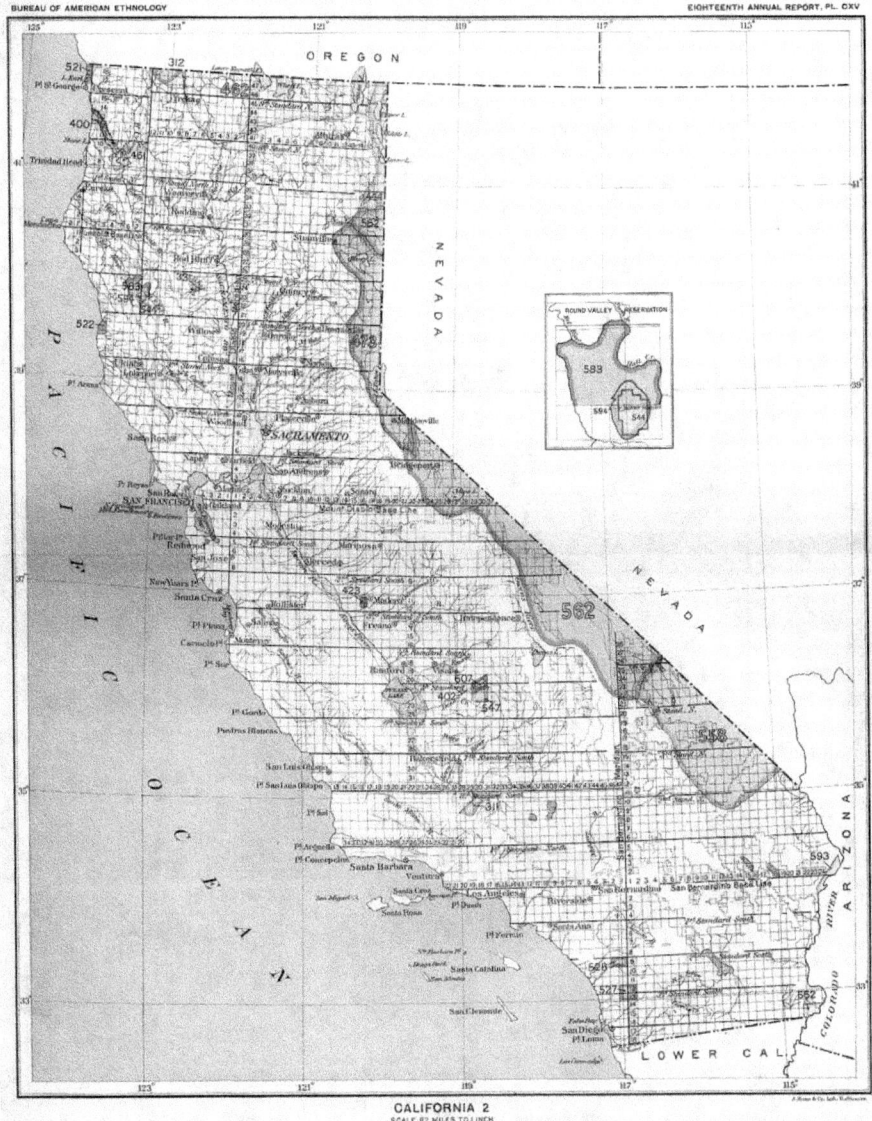

CALIFORNIA 2
SCALE 62 MILES TO 1 INCH

29

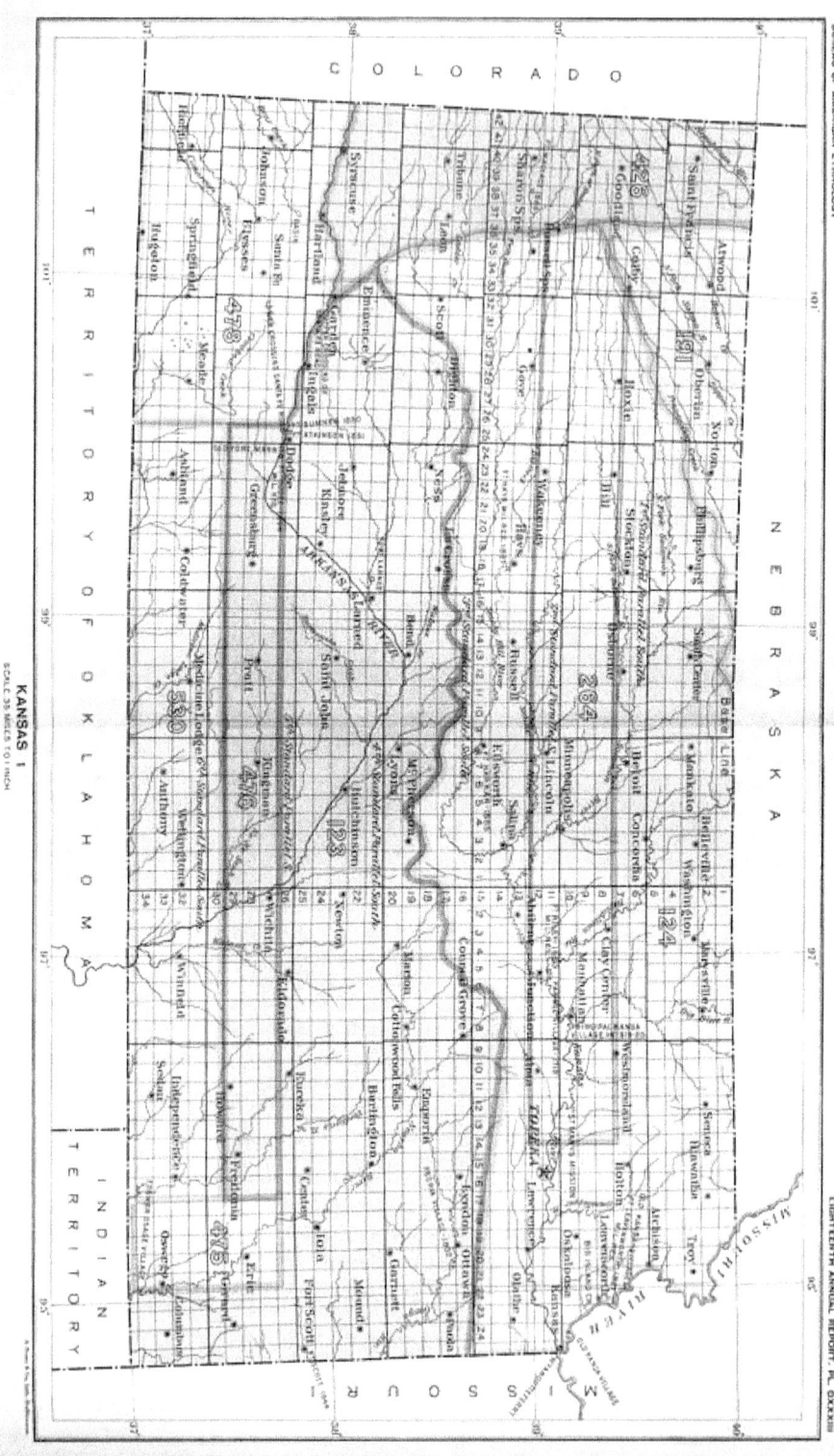

**KANSAS** 1

SCALE 35 MILES TO 1 INCH

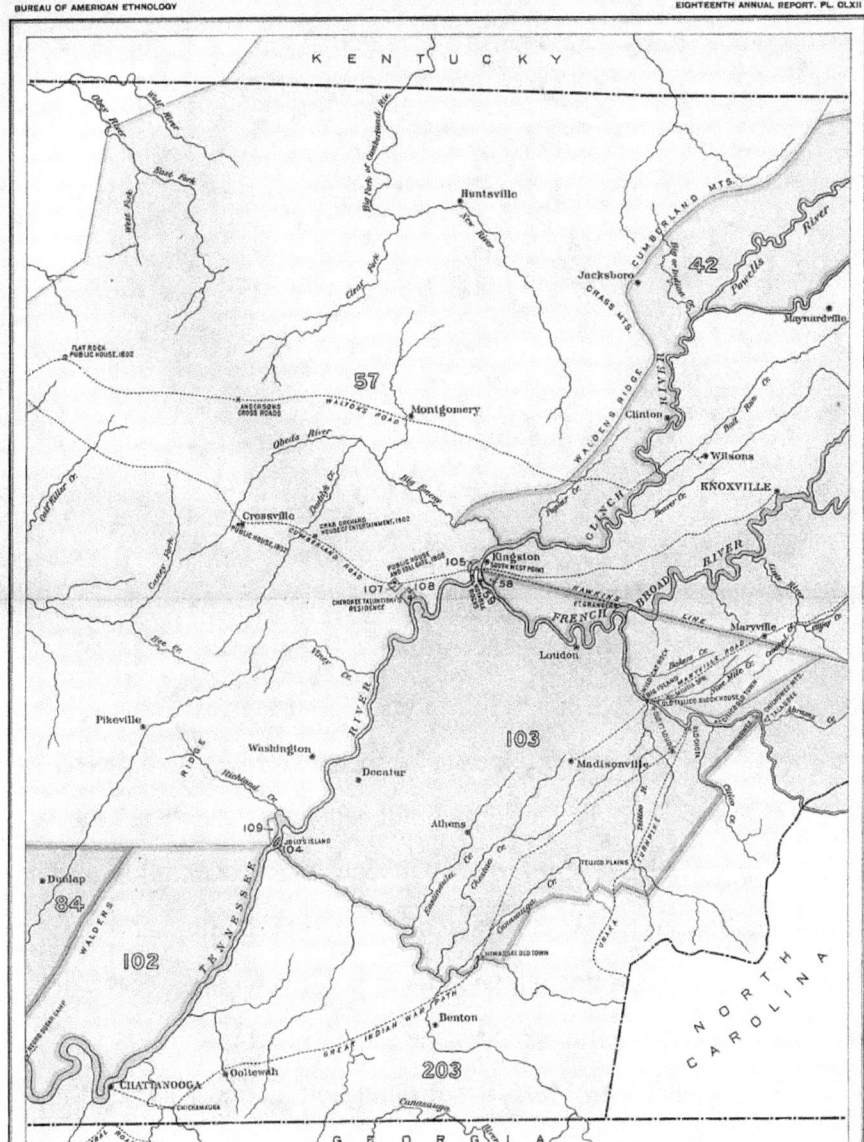

TENNESSEE (DETAIL)
SCALE, 10 MILES TO 1 INCH

# *Chapter Three*

## *Looking For Connections*

*Charles American Horse, Library of Congress*

University students working on their PhDs do us a great service when they submit their work to the Internet, especially when it comes to sociology and culture. For example, independent researchers who share their research see similarities between Japanese and Polynesian artwork and that of the Northwest Coastal Indians. Cotton strains, games, sculptures and boats give hints of possible contact between South America and cultures across the seas, like China, Egypt and Africa. The pyramids in Mesoamerica and South America are another example. And Egypt's Nile River agricultural methods may have influenced the Mississippi River cultures.

Ancient Middle Eastern cultures may have contributed to the languages of the Southwestern Indians as well as the languages of the tribes along America's Eastern Atlantic Coast. I've seen postings in genealogical message boards where the poster insists they see Hebrew

32

inscriptions at ancient North American sites. And there are similarities between the Mississippi area inscriptions to those of ancient Egypt. In the eastern United States, there are historical markers with etchings that are close to those of early Celtic tribes who lived in what's now Spain and Portugal.

Many spots in the eastern United States draw the attention of history buffs. There are Stonehenge type rocks that were placed there eons ago, leaving those appreciating them to wonder, why is this an historical site in Ireland and in America it's been scoffed off as a root cellar? And some see strong connections between the languages of ancient Phoenicians and those of Native American tribes. The Melungeons have an oral legend that they descend from shipwrecked Portuguese sailors and Phoenicians are also mentioned in their oral history. The Basque may have made it to ancient America as well.

Here are the top fifty *American* Indian and *Alaskan Native* surnames derived from the U.S. Census Bureau in 2000: JOHNSON, BEGAY, YAZZIE, LOCKLEAR, JONES, WILLIAMS, BROWN, DAVIS, WILSON, THOMPSON, THOMAS, MILLER, JACKSON, WHITE, MARTIN, LEE, HUNT, JAMES, LEWIS, TAYLOR, ANDERSON, CLARK, GARCIA, MARTINEZ, BENALLY, SCOTT, TSOSIE, MOORE, NELSON, KING, JACOBS, OXENDINE, WALKER, NEZ, HARRIS, ALLEN, HILL, MITCHELL, PHILLIPS, JOHN, BAKER, YOUNG, ADAMS, CHAVIS, MORGAN, ROBERTS, HALL, LOPEZ, WRIGHT. (See the rest of the list here: http://names.mongabay.com/data/indians.html)

As much as I'd like to be positive, I have to address the issue that for some of us, our American Indian ancestry came into our European family trees through force. I hate to say that but it's true. I've read accounts where women were given away as gifts. But the past is the past and if you're anything like me, you're proud of all your ancestry, known and unknown and want to know the whole truth.

When the Russians came down the west coast to get furs, they would sail to a Native village, descend upon it, oftentimes violently. They gave fur traps to the men and threatened to harm their women and children if they did not deliver furs to them. Once the Indian males left to hunt the furs to pay the ransom and gain the release of their families, the Russian men treated the Indian women like concubines. These intruders often followed through on their threats and murdered family members of those Indians who did not return with enough furs. Once the Russians obtained a good number of furs they would finally leave but the fear that they would return (which they did) was always on the minds of the Natives.

*Quote*

The Iroquois of New York had progressed beyond any other Native people north of Mexico in the elaboration of a state and empire. Through a carefully planned system of confederations, originating about 1570, the five allied tribes had secured internal peace and unity, by which they had been able to acquire dominant control over most of the tribes from Hudson Bay to Carolina, and if not prematurely checked by the advent of the whites, might in time have founded a northern empire to rival that of the Aztec. **New Advent, Catholic Encyclopedia** http://www.newadvent.org/cathen/07747a.htm

If you believe your ancestor was Indian because you saw a picture of them dressed in Native clothing and they belonged to the "Honorable Order of Red Men," please be aware that this was not a Native organization, in fact Indians were excluded from the Order. It's easy to see how someone could make that mistake but be careful. The white men who founded this organization and those who join, base their rituals on Native traditions. Besides Native clothing, the Order uses sign language and Indian names. It sounds like they imitate Indians. They have a council fire and hold meetings in a tepee. Easy to see how anyone could be confused by this. The women's group is called "Pocahontas." I know very little about either of these groups. One never knows about groups that have been around for ages. Perhaps the original members had Native ancestry and they were confused about their identity. I really don't know but my understanding is the Honorable Order of Red Men is *not* a Native American Secret Society.

It wasn't until recently that I thought about pipe smoking as a clue to Native ancestry. Believing that your grandfather was Indian because he smoked a pipe? How ridiculous is that? Perhaps not at all. It doesn't hurt to think about that. There were ceremonial smoking clubs and pipe clubs. My grandfather, who my brother said was Indian, smoked a pipe. And if you're looking for it, he looked Indian.

I've seen it written that an Indian marriage may not have been in a church. Good point. So if you run across a discrepancy of the marriage date, one through church records the other not, that could be what's going on and a wonderful clue.

In a Native American forum, someone posted that a university study revealed a high percentage of Americans surveyed said they were of some Cherokee descent and how statistically impossible that would be. On another entirely different Native American forum, someone posted that the Indians of other tribes were saying that they were Cherokee because people were less afraid of Cherokees. Cherokee Indians had a reputation of being friendly to Europeans.

*Quote*
The practice of Cherokee and other Southeast Indians identifying as "Black Dutch" seemed to originate during and after the 1830s Indian Removal era. They used this term to explain their dark looks and to avoid being removed to Indian Territory or stigmatized by what became a majority Anglo-American society. Some Native Americans, mainly from the Five Civilized Tribes of the Southeast, claimed

"Black Dutch" or "Black Irish" heritage to purchase land in areas which United States treaties and other laws had reserved for people of European descent. Once they owned the land, such families who had escaped forced removal would not admit to their American Indian heritage, for fear of losing their property.

**Black Dutch - Wikipedia, the free encyclopedia**

en.wikipedia.org/wiki/Black_Dutch

In the late 1700's Colonists left the East Coast and ventured over the Appalachians. That was going west for them. They encountered great Indian resistance. Eventually, in 1825, pockets of Indian land were made into reservations and "Indian Country" was officially between the Red River and the Missouri River. Then five years later the *Indian Removal Act* relocated more Natives (Eastern Indians) to Indian Country. Then, due in large part to the building of railroads, the Homestead Act and the Civil War, Indian Country shrunk, a lot. In 1854, the northern part of Indian Country became the Kansas and Nebraska Territories. Kansas's northern border is Nebraska and its southern border is Oklahoma. *We're talking Indian Country.* If you were always told that your ancestor was born in Kansas or Nebraska but they were born before 1854, they were born in Indian Country.

Before the U.S. Government started chopping up and surveying Indian land, Europeans began squatting in Indian Country. They would find a spot they thought would make a suitable home site and build a home and plant crops. (We may find both Indians and squatters in our family trees.) Many of the squatters were able to stay because of laws that were in their favor because they had been living on the land. Eventually, developers saw Indian land as an opportunity for prosperity so pressed the United States government to release Indian land for development. The government agreed and even though there were treaties protecting Indian land, they went ahead and surveyed it into tracts. They abandoned certain treaties, changed the laws and some Indians became landowners. This freed up two million acres that was sold really cheap by the Indian landowners to squatters and others. What was left of Indian Country became part of the state of Oklahoma.

*Quote*

"The Cherokee migration of 1838-39 came to be called the "Trail of Tears." The name now stands for the forced removals and suffering of the various Southeast tribes, and by extension, the forced relocation of tribes of the Old Northwest and all other displaced Indians."
Carl Waldman
**Atlas of The North American Indian**

There are very few federal or state reservations in the eastern United States. They are mostly in the northern Midwest and the west. The southwest has large reservation land holdings, the Navajo reservation consists of 14 million acres.

*Quote*

According to Cones Kupwah - Snowflower many early Ohio "white" settlers, were hidden Native Americans who moved west as the whites approached. The people of many Nations who were with Tecumseh at

38

the Battle of the Thames (1813) were automatically considered outlaws, and not allowed to return home. As it became harder for them to live in exile, they filtered back in twos, threes, sometimes whole families. The English Quakers and German Amish took them in, protected them, often claiming them as family members... Also, in 1832 were 600 Shawnee on the Wapakoneta Reservation in north western Ohio, when the Army showed up and ordered them to pack and leave. 300 arrived at the first Shawnee reservation, in what was to become Kansas City Mo. What about the others? Well, they went far enough away, where they thought no one would recognize them and changed their appearance. If they spoke fluent English, they claimed to be English. If they spoke broken English - German or Dutch.

Laurie Beth Duffy

http://imblackeagle.tripod.com/looks1.htm


## What Physical Characteristics Do Native Americans Share?

### Blood Types

Many American Indians have blood type O. I have blood type O. I also have the Rh-negative blood factor and so do a lot of Basques. But so do other groups like Oriental Jews of Israel and Ancient Iranian Jews, as well as Berbers. So I assumed that I had an ancestor who was from one of these ethnicities before coming to the New World. But while reading, "Atlas of the North American Indian," by Carl Waldman, I see that researchers have found similarities in the language of Native Americans as well as grave markers, in Pennsylvania and the Gulf of St. Lawrence, that resemble those of the Basque ethnic group. So the Basque may have come to America a very long time ago and it is through a Basque Native American ancestor that I've inherited this blood factor. It is a very ancient connection and one that is intriguing, adding more to that elusive history of the Rh-negative factor.

*Quote*
The highest percentage of type O (57%) was found in Hispanic donors (a group that includes donors of Mexican, Puerto Rican, and Cuban descent). The next highest percentage of type O was found in North American Indian (55%) and black (50%) donors.
*Blood Groups and Red Cell Antigens*
**National Center for Biotechnology Information**
**U.S. National Library of Medicine**

While browsing the Internet I repeatedly ran across similar dialogues regarding physical characteristics of Native Americans. Many contradict one another and there isn't a one of us that can't find a physical attribute we share with Natives. But here's what I gathered up. It's not scientific but it is interesting.

Face: long, well-rounded, large, flat, broad, high cheekbones
Skin: fair, yellowish, light brown, red, pale, black, copper, white, caramel, newborns have a birthmark type blue stain
Hair: straight, a little coarse, silky, shiny, black, reddish, rarely bald
Eyes: not as wide open as in the general population, hazel, dark brown, oriental, brown, ring around the iris, fat eyelids, long thick eyelashes, slanted, almond shape, lazy eye in children, eyelids have extra fold, far-sighted

Men's Facial Hair: scant, not as heavy as in the general population, grows between the eyebrows, thick and long

Fingernails: strong, tinge of blue

Nose: aquiline (men), short base then wide, narrow, straight

Lips: average

Ears: thick, large heavy earlobes

Neck: not thin or long

Chest: large

Calves: smaller than general population

Hands: smaller than general population, crooked fingers, crooked little finger

Feet: small, extra bone ridge on outside

Toes: short toes that separate, big toe shorter than the second toe, wide space between big toe and second toe

Chin: high, symmetrical

Teeth: gap in front teeth, large front teeth, concave shovel shaped upper incisors, modest canines, carrabelli cusp missing on maxillary first molars, bony nodes protruding from jaw bone under tongue

Humerus, Femur and Tibia: often flat

Height: short, tall, average

Shape: round, stout, sturdy, broad shoulders, muscular, stocky, strong, corpulent

Breastbone: inverted

Blood: uncommon antigens


There are also diseases that are prevalent among Native Americans:

Alcoholism: absence of the enzyme necessary to digest alcohol

Arthritis - degenerative arthritis, juvenile rheumatoid arthritis

Fibromyalgia

Diabetes

Crossed eyes

Glaucoma

Chronic muscle pain

Excess iron in the bloodstream

Kidney disease

Lactose Intolerance

Cardiovascular disease

Endometriosis

Esophageal achalasia: inability of smooth muscle to move food down the esophagus

Thyroid problems

Gall bladder problems

Hearing loss: for more info see

http://www.cherokeephoenix.org/20196/Article.aspx

*Quote*

Over the thousands of years that indigenous peoples have lived in the Americas, they have developed into a great number of local populations, each differing somewhat from its neighbors. Some populations (such as those on the Great Plains of North America) tend to be tall and often heavy in build, whereas others (for example, many in the South American Andes and adjacent lowlands) tend to be short and broad chested; furthermore, every population includes persons who vary from the average. Some physical characteristics of Native American populations have been influenced by diet or by the environmental conditions of their societies. For example, the short stature of some Native Guatemalans seems to result at least in part from diets poor in protein; the broad chests and large hearts and lungs of Native Andeans represent an adaptation to the low-oxygen atmosphere of the high mountains they inhabit.

**Contributed by: Sandra L. CadwaladerContributed by: Sandra L. Cadwalader**

http://autocww2.colorado.edu/~toldy2/E64ContentFiles/HistoryOfThe Americas/NativeAmericans.htm

# Chapter Four
## Lonely Frontiersmen

Timothy Flint's, *The History and Geography of the Mississippi Valley,* (1833) speaks of young Frenchmen and their pursuit to "ascend the long rivers for furs and peltries, and to negotiate marriages. When they returned, dances and copious narratives of their adventures and exploits signalized their holiday of repose." And of the early settlers of Louisiana Flint writes, "The lower classes had their dogs and guns, and Indian beauties... It was perhaps a fortunate trait in their character, certainly an amiable one, that they were so easy in forming new associations with the savages, the only companions they could expect in these remote deserts, where they heard from France seldom more than once in a year. Their descendants, who inhabit these regions, speak of their fathers as a favored race of mortals, and of those times as a golden age..."

*Quote*

The Métis are descendants of marriages of Woodland Cree, Ojibway, Saulteaux, and Menominee aboriginals to French Canadians, Scots and English, and are one of three recognized Aboriginal peoples in Canada. (pronounced "MAY-tee" or "may-TEE" in English, they are also historically known as Bois Brule, mixed-bloods, Countryborn (or Anglo-Métis). Their homeland consists of the Canadian provinces of British Columbia, Alberta, Saskatchewan, Manitoba, and Ontario, as well as the Northwest Territories. The Métis Homeland also includes parts of the northern United States (specifically Montana, North Dakota, and northwest Minnesota).

http://gelineau-homepage.com/gen_8A.htm

Who hasn't heard of the French-Canadian fur trappers with their fringy jackets and canoes? These men are a part of American history, beginning in the 1600's and before, when Frenchmen were either recruited by the Catholic Church or explorers like Champlain, who with money from royals and aristocratic speculators, lived in the thick forests of the North. To say these fur trappers and traders were hearty would be an understatement.

In many instances the Natives probably taught the frontiersmen the best techniques to trap animals. These hearty men also married the sisters and daughters of the Indians they'd become acquainted with, bringing Native ancestry into one's family tree. A Native American woman, who spoke in her Native tongue and had the knowledge of hunting and terrain, was an asset to a frontiersman, especially if she kept her connections with tribal members.

French-Canadian woodsmen were also known as *voyageurs* and *coureurs de bois*. (The courerus de bois were also mail carriers between Quebec and Halifax.) When a voyageur or a coureurs de bois married an Indian sister or daughter, very often from the Cree tribe, their descendants were known as Metis. When we speak of Metis today, we may be including a much larger Native population into the culture, but originally the *Metis* were people whose parents or grandparents were both French and Cree.

*Bois Brule* is another French-Canadian title that is used to describe someone of "mixed blood." The French word brules means *burnt* and bois means *wood*. So *bois brule* means *burnt wood*. It's easy to imagine how that nickname came about. These frontiersmen must have come out of the woods smelling like campfires.

Another title given, this time to women, was *Casquette girls*. Cloaked, hooded, and carrying a trunk on her back that included a wedding dress, French girls were brought to Louisiana in the earliest years of 1700 to marry French Colonists. Because the Frenchmen were marrying Indian women, frowned on by their military officers, the French government believed the Casquette girls would prevent that. At first, it was just twenty young girls but the numbers grew to 500. Although the girls were protected by nuns who traveled along with them until they found proper husbands, their lives in France had not been as sheltered. The Casquette girls were recruited from prisons, brothels and orphanages in France.

Because there were almost no women in the Pacific Northwest at the time of the Civil War, women were highly sought after. And because the war made widows out of many young women, women made the trip out west to become brides for lonely frontiersmen. By the time the Civil War came about, a mountain man could have been the descendant of a frontiersman *and* an Indian woman. The mountain man then married one of the "brides" who came over the Oregon Trail. It may have been long forgotten (or purposely forgotten) that he had an Indian ancestor.

Another thought is that our Indian ancestors could very well be the children or grandchildren of those forced into slavery. Some tribes had large slave populations and slaves were taken in raids then ransomed back to their families. Sometimes very young children, teens and women were bought from other tribes and from raiders and traders. "Captured Shoshone Maiden" was an expression I read in one history book. And some will tell you that the term "squaw" is a derogatory name given to Indian women by the French.

Because of intermarrying between Indian tribes, there exists a "melting pot." Although it would be nice, *really* nice, to know which tribes our ancestors originally belonged to, we would at least like to confirm that they were indeed Native people. When researching the Metis, I read a thesis paper by J. Elizabeth Sperry, an anthropologist at the University of Montana that sheds a light on the nomadic nature of Canadian Indians, keeping the thought in mind that there was no ocean separating Canada from the United States. The Metis people are descendants of the northern tribes and although you may see Cree mentioned as the dominant Metis tribe, Sperry tells us that "... Metis, Cree, and Chippewa maintained a network of social kinship across Montana. Many lived on existing reservations with friends and relatives and intermarried among members of various tribes." Sperry's writing is enlightening and reminds us that a Canadian Indian can also be an American Indian, depending on what time of year they were hunting and gathering. In later years, they were migrant workers, a "landless people" who experienced great difficulty when the new European culture changed everything. Also mentioned with the Metis, Cree and Chippewa were the Crow, Northern Cheyenne, Salish-Kutenai (Flathead), and Blackfeet.

There are a lot of birth, baptism, marriage and death records found among the Canadian Catholic churches. If you're lucky, you might find the rare instance where an original Native name is listed, but like other European cultures, it was important for the "authorities" to convert the Natives. Your great-great-grandfather may have been *Running Fox* but most of the original Indian names are long forgotten. His new name became something like, Francois de Geoffroy or Pierre Boudereau. We could be staring at a European name on our family tree and not realize he was Indian. Many genealogists insist that we prove everything but it's your family tree, if you have an intelligent hunch that you can guess which ancestor may have been the Indian in your family, make those notations, you can always say, "this is my gut feeling based on the year, the location and bits and pieces of family lore."

The French were comfortable intermarrying with Natives but adamantly opposed to assimilating with and adopting English culture. The French-Canadian and Metis from the area that is now Nova Scotia were called Acadians, because before the English changed the name of the territory it was called Acadia. These Acadians wanted ***no part*** in English culture. They had their own wonderful way of life, culturally different from the English. The English tried persuading them to pledge allegiance to their monarchy but the Acadians refused. Eventually the English cruelly drove the Acadians from their homes. Families were separated and many died of diseases on the ships that sent them to Caribbean Islands. But the Acadians found their way into Louisiana in the 1700s and have a strong culture there today. The region is called Acadiana and the people refer to themselves as Cajuns and Creoles. My point is, Acadians have an extensive Native history.

The word *Cajun* is the corrupted form of Acadian. Today, in Louisiana a person who is of Acadian French descent is affectionately (I hope) known as a Cajun. A *Creole* is a person of French or Spanish descent born and reared in a colonial or remote region, especially an intertropical region. OR: In the United States, a white person descended from the French or Spanish settlers of Louisiana and the Gulf States and preserving their characteristic speech and culture. OR: A black person born in America.

Sept 5th, 1755 is the day of *Le Grand Derangement.* The Acadian farmers (in what later became Nova Scotia) were arrested and packed into English ships. They were separated from their families and in many instances their homes were burnt to the ground. Half the Acadians died on the ship, from diseases spreading from immigrants the English were bringing over to populate "Nova Scotia" (formerly Acadia).

After the Acadians were expelled from their homeland, some Acadian families continued on in small villages along the St John's River in what the English began to call "New Brunswick." History shows a **tight relationship between French settlers and their Native connections** in the lower St John's Valley. This relationship is what helped them to survive.

The English continued to harass the Acadians, who would not pledge allegiance to the British monarchy. They continued burning Acadian villages. The Acadians knew the forests well and lived in them during the Seven Years War, from 1756 to 1763.

In 1755, the French still controlled the Mississippi river and the great resource it provided. The Seven Years War was all about changing that. For seven years the French and the British fought a war. The Choctaw Indians were allied with the French and the Chickasaw Indians allied with the British. Even though the British won the war and gained control over the vast Mississippi territory, Louisiana still proudly retains a strong French history and culture. And because Spain had times of control as well, this mixture of ethnicities provides for a wonderful cultural experience that Cajuns are quite proud of, especially those whose ancestors have been there since the 1700's.

In 1763 three world powers, Britain, France and Spain signed the *Treaty of Paris* and halted the Seven Year's War. Spain lost territory because she helped France, so Spain was given New Orleans and all the French territory between the Mississippi and the Rockies. (In 1801

France took it back.) The treaty also addressed the Acadians who had been forcibly removed from their lands. Many Acadians went home only to find that English farmers had moved onto their property. The Acadians were told they were welcome to work for the new farmers but they must pledge allegiance to the British monarchy. Acadians who went to Canada were also required to pledge allegiance to the British monarchy. Many Acadians found their way to Illinois through Louisiana bringing Metis ancestry to Louisiana, Mississippi, Illinois and territories surrounding those states. Going through Canada into Illinois would have been dangerous because the English controlled Canada.

This all sounds familiar because when I was in Kentucky, searching my own genealogy, a Dutch genealogist told me that the Low Dutch of Kentucky kept running from the English because they didn't want their children to be "English." There was a very out-spoken Frenchman living amongst the Low Dutch of my family, he undoubtedly had a powerful influence upon the Kentucky colony.

The British wanted to populate the territories they took from the Acadians so allowed a lot of Scottish immigrants into Nova Scotia. This is probably when many Scottish people began to intermarry with Indians and also slaves who found freedom in Canada. There are plenty of Metis who have Scottish and English ancestry. My husband does. His family has this great oral history. One of the women in his family was born of aristocratic English ancestry. She ran off with a French-Canadian-Indian who played the fiddle. Her English family disowned her. I searched for over thirty years to find this history. I finally found a lot of it but it is so ornamented with French that it's hard to find the Indian or Indians in the family tree. I had never heard of the word Metis until a few years ago, now it's one of the reasons I'm writing this book, that and my own quest to find my Native ancestry.

*Quote*

"It is known that many Africans intermarried with Native Americans. Less widely known is the fact that many Native Americans also owned African slaves, and fathered children with African slave women. In addition, there were smaller numbers [of] Free People of Color who lived in many of the nations and who also lived and married persons from the same nations, and whose descendants claim ancestry from the Oklahoma Black Indian people. As a result, thousands of Americans have African and Indian ancestry."

http://www.Nativeweb.org/resources/genealogy_tracing_roots_/

# Chapter Five

## Belonging to a Tribe

*Charging Thunder Indian Man & Woman, Library of Congress*

*Quote*

Good Fox said the popular perception of Native Americans is rooted in stereotypes –the idea that a "real Indian" looks and acts a certain way, and that anyone who doesn't conform to that image is somehow "less Indian." But the truth is more diverse –different tribes can have different physical characteristics, and intermarriage among other ethnic groups mean that Native Americans often have a multiracial background.

Stephanie Siek, **CNN**

http://inamerica.blogs.cnn.com/2012/05/14/whos-a-Native-american-its-complicated/

Millions of people have Native American ancestry. You don't need someone's permission to have that blood running through your veins but if you want to claim a spot on a tribal registry, you must jump through several hoops, which means you have to prove to them that your ancestor was originally a tribal member. If your ancestor was Cherokee but went their own way when the white settlers finally gained control, don't waste your time. You'll not find them listed on any tribal registry. It gets terribly confusing so let me simplify it by comparing it to an organization. Let's say the US government decided to make an organization out of Indians who were left after Indian wars and forced removals. For various reasons, the government decided it was best to create this organization. The government put the word out that they were allocating land to Indians who joined the organization and those who were tribal members came forward and said yes, they wanted to join the organization, and got on the list (roll). Others said, heck no, I'll just keep telling everyone I'm Black Dutch (or Black German, etc.) and I'll work hard and farm some land. Your ancestor didn't join the organization or wasn't accepted? Forget about wasting your time finding them on the registry.

The rolls were created by The Bureau of Indian Affairs (BIA). It's confusing because in their paperwork they say they formerly maintained those rolls but no longer do. But they also say that the names of those who are on today's tribal rolls are protected by a "Privacy Act" and that the BIA maintains them. So I guess they do and they don't. Perhaps the key word here is *maintain*. The BIA publishes a Tribal Leaders Directory of the 562 tribes. After reading up on the BIA, here are some tips for identifying an ancestor:

1) If an individual is not currently a member of a federally recognized tribe, band or group, research should begin in non-Indian records or other public records such as those records maintained by state and

local governments, like county courthouse records (deeds, wills, land or property conveyances), churches, and schools.

2) The most important information is vital statistics, including ancestral names, dates of birth, marriages (or divorces) and the places where ancestors were born, lived, married, and died. (Birth, death and marriage records.)

3) Formerly the BIA created and maintained tribal rolls. Today, Federal policies limit BIA involvement in tribal membership matters. It would take Congress or a tribal order for the BIA to become involved in these issues. That said, if your ancestors had land in trust or went through probate, a BIA field office where your ancestor resided may have some records concerning ancestry. They DO NOT MAINTAIN RECORDS OF ALL INDIVIDUALS WHO POSSESS SOME DEGREE OF INDIAN BLOOD.

4) If you have the *specifics* on your ancestor (name, birth date and their relation to you) you can contact one of the BIA field offices to see if they have any documents pertaining to your ancestor.

Where can we obtain vital statistic documents (birth certificates, death certificates, marriage licenses, etc.)? You should be able to find them at the Bureau of Vital Statistics in the state where your ancestor was born, died, or owned property, etc. Look for this bureau at the state capital. If it is before 1890 they won't have any records because they didn't keep them yet. Even up to 1915 they may not have them. I'm sure there is a cost for obtaining records. Call the Bureau or look up their website to find the cost. After finding the cost, here's an example of a letter you could write, requesting records:

Hello,

I am a genealogist looking for records on my grandfather, John Doe. He was born in Memphis, Tennessee on February 15, 1918. Please send me any and all records relating to my grandfather, including birth, death, marriage or divorce.

Thank you,

Mary Doe (Include your address, phone number and email address.)

As I stated above, before 1915 the states didn't keep records but the National Archives in Washington, D.C. has census records from as early as 1790. They may be on microfilm and they are available at a price. (For more on the National Archives see Chapter Eight: The Rolls and the Rules.)

*Quote*

"And contrary to popular belief, individual Indians do not automatically receive federal funds simply because they are Indians. Types and sources of funds vary from tribe to tribe - income from leasing or development of tribal property and resources; federal compensation for treaty violations, encroachments on Indian lands and mismanagement of trust property and funds; or subsidies from special government programs."

Carl Waldman, **Atlas of The North American Indian**

Some of the federally recognized tribes require that you have a *Certificate of Degree of Indian Blood*, CDIB. This is obtained after you prove your Native American ancestry. Requirements for the different tribes vary but there is no quantum blood requirement to become a member of the Cherokee Nation, quantum means "how much."

*Quote*

The Bureau of Indian Affairs has used a "blood quantum" definition—generally, one-fourth degree of American Indian "blood"—and/or tribal membership to recognize a person as an American Indian. However, each tribe has a particular set of requirements, typically including a blood quantum, for membership (enrollment) in the tribe. Requirements vary widely from tribe to tribe: a few tribes require at least a one-half Indian (or tribal) blood quantum; many others require a one-fourth blood quantum; still others, generally in California and Oklahoma, require a one-eighth, one-sixteenth, or one-thirty-second blood quantum; and some tribes have no minimum blood quantum requirement at all but require an explicitly documented tribal lineage.
Roy Cook

**Heart of Colonialism Bleeds Blood Quantum**

http://www.americanindiansource.com/bloodquantum.html

NOTE: See Chapter Seven *"Searching the Dawes Final Roll"* for more information about belonging to a tribe.

## Chapter Six

## *The Rolls and the Rules*

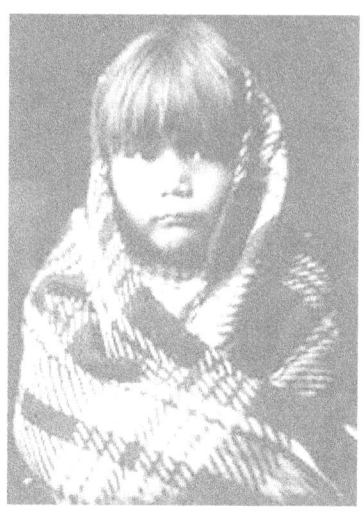

*Navaho Child, Library of Congress*

*"A beautiful soft blanket woven from the furs of rabbits and child's sandals made from sagebrush fibers were found preserved for close to 10,000 years in a cool, dry cave." Burns Paiute Tribe, Oregon http://www.burnspaiute-nsn.gov/*

I asked my husband what he'd like to see in this book and he said, a surname index. "I want to go to the back of the book and look up an ancestor's surname." I laughed, wishing it were that simple. I suppose if you're related to a famous Native American that information is available. For the majority of us, we have to do the work.

The beginning of Indian lists probably began in the early days of European encroachment when missionaries, hunters, explorers and traders kept lists of the names of the Native people that they either controlled, feared or did business with. As European settlement advanced, any lists of Natives were kept by the local authorities of those settlements and then later, by militias and army administrators.

The information in this chapter is complicated and confusing. Please read through the whole chapter before taking any of the suggested steps. It isn't easy to take a complex system of Indian tribes and find an ancestor among them.

My head spins when I think of large territories and how they were broken into smaller states. Missouri Territory split off creating Arkansas. Arkansas Territory held what is today's Oklahoma. Old records might list Georgia as your ancestor's birthplace but today's Georgia encompasses a much smaller area and territories that were formerly Georgia have become new states. The history of Indian territories is also confusing. The government made treaties, relocated Indians, broke treaties and relocated them again. The Biblical expression *Diaspora* comes to mind and is used frequently when discussing Native American history.

The word "enumeration" has to do with tallying up, much like what Moses did. In the "Fourth Book of Moses," known in the Bible as the "Book of Numbers," in Numbers 26 you'll see that Reuben, the eldest son of Jacob (Israel) is asked by Moses and Eleazar to "take the sum of the people." They begin an inventory and soon Hanoch's children become Hanochites, Pallu's children become Palluites, Hezron's children become Hezronites and Carmi's children become Carmites. The U.S. Government took a similar inventory of Indians.

After many years of colonial expansion, the federal government decided to make "enumerations" of the remaining Indians. The "enumerations" are now called lists, rolls or schedules, sometimes named after the fellow whose job it was to create the list. Some of the lists were lost and some were never taken. It's a good thing Native Americans have a tradition of oral history because sometimes that's all that's left. Not all tribes are represented in the lists, leaving out a lot of ancestors we're trying to find.

Before 1790 there were no censuses. Between 1790-1840 Indians were not listed on a federal census. 1860 was the first year that Indians living in the general population were tallied on the federal census. Unfortunately, large portions of the 1890 census schedules were destroyed in a fire but *not all were destroyed.* By 1900, Indians from the general population and those living on reservations were counted, or "enumerated."

1850 was the first thorough census that recorded the whole family. According to the National Archives, during this time period, "most of the mid-West" was Indian Country where they had not yet taken any censuses. By 1860 Indian Country had become Oklahoma and a census was taken there but the Indians weren't counted for the general census, although an Indian census is found on roll 52 of the Arkansas census. On rare occasions, you may find "I" or "In" listed in the 1860 general census but you probably won't find them listed in the general census until 1870. The 1900 census is important, the National Archives notes the following:

"Indians on reservations and in the general population are identified in column 5, Color or Race. A special Indian schedule added additional questions to the general schedule. Special Indian schedules usually are found at the end of the county, but sometimes grouped together on last roll of microfilm for the state. Indians living with non-Indian families outside of reservations were enumerated on general schedule with those families. There was a census of Indian Territory (Oklahoma) taken."

By 1910, Indians are listed along with everyone else but there was a "Special Indian Schedule" that had extra questions and those are found in the county where they resided. There were no special Indian schedules for the 1920 census, they were counted with everyone else. Nor were there any special Indian schedules for the 1930 census but they do begin asking the "degree of Indian blood."

Here are some important rolls. Some include a link. Once you get to that website, **watch where you scroll. There is often an extra search field aimed at steering you away from that website.** Usually you scroll down toward the bottom to find the free search field.

**Reservation Rolls** - 1817. This is a list of applicants for 640 acre land tracts offered to accepted applicants instead of going to Arkansas. It was really more of a lease because when the person died, the acreage was returned back to the state if there were no heirs. The majority of the applicants were denied. Read the list here:
http://tngenweb.org/records/tn_wide/history/first/1817cherokee.pdf

**1817 Cherokee Emigration Rolls**: When Southeastern and Georgia Cherokees were "removed" to the western side of the Mississippi River they were documented. These lists contain diverse information. Contact the National Archives to view the records.

**Armstrong Rolls** - 1831. Each Choctaw head of a family who wishes to become a citizen of the United States was asked to apply and if accepted would receive land and so would the children. This link will take you to the Armstrong Roll. Scroll down to the bottom, going past the ancestry.com search field and any other search field. Look for "Search the Armstrong Rolls."
http://www.accessgenealogy.com/Native/armstrong-rolls.htm

**1835 Henderson Roll:** After a treaty, the Cherokees gave up their land east of the Mississippi River and were moved to Oklahoma "Indian Country." The Henderson Roll is a listing of 16,000 Cherokees who lived in North Carolina, Georgia, Tennessee and Alabama. This removal to Oklahoma is known as the "Trail of Tears." View the lists of names here: http://www.accessgenealogy.com/native/1835-henderson-roll.htm

**1850-1870 New Mexico Territory Censuses: Pueblo Indians**
The United States Census Bureau has these censuses. They can be found here:
https://www.census.gov/history/www/genealogy/decennial_census_rec ords/censuses_of_american_indians.html

**Siler Roll 1851 (Eastern Cherokee):**

An enumeration taken by a man named Siler. He took the names and added extra information. The names are of families who received a payment. These families lived in Georgia, Washington D.C., Tennessee and North Carolina. This list contains about 1,700 names. The only place I found it online required I join AOL (America Online). Here is the link: http://lifestream.aol.com/

**Drennen Rolls 1852:** A roll of Cherokee names who were forced to leave and walk to Oklahoma in 1839, the "Trail of Tears." Search for names here: http://www.accessgenealogy.com/native/drennen-rolls.htm (Scroll down to the second search box.)

**Chapman Roll** - Named after Albert Chapman, the man who in 1852 compiled the list. This list of names is important because those who had ancestry on this list were then granted their name on the Guion Miller Roll in 1910. This list is on microfilm available at the National Archives. You can view some of the list here, many of the names are authentic Native names:

http://www.tngennet.org/cherokee_by_blood/chapman.htm

**1857 Shawnee Census: Part of the Kansas Territorial Censuses, 1855-1859** (at the end of roll 1 of the 1857 census is a census of Shawnee Indians in Kansas Territory). This can be found on Microfilm reel K-1 at the Kansas State Historical Society and through the National Archives.

**1860 Slave Census:** Ancestry.com has the *1860 U.S. Federal Census - Slave Schedules* online. It's very easy to search surnames:

http://search.ancestry.com/search/db.aspx?dbid=7668

**1871 Shawnee Census:**

In 1866 the United States finalized a treaty with the Cherokees and within that treaty, the Shawnee Tribe and the Cherokee Nation of Indians entered into an agreement. This census is the list of names of the Shawnee tribe who relocated to Indian Territory (the Cherokee Nation) between June 9th, 1869 and June 10th, 1871. View the census here: http://www.accessgenealogy.com/native/1871-shawnee-census.htm

**1880 Special Census of Indians:** This is a list of Indians in Washington Territory, Dakota Territory, and California. A bit of information is given as well as names. This census is available through the National Archives. The census ID number is M1791.

**Wallace Roll:** *Cherokee Freedmen in Indian Territory, 1890.*

Due to the fact that Cherokees had slaves and these "Negroes" had been living within the tribe and probably intermarried within the tribe, this roll was established having to do with a treaty made with the government one year after the Civil War ended. The Wallace Roll is named after John W. Wallace, the man who took the tally of "Rejected Freedmen, Free Negroes, Authenticated and Admitted" Cherokee Indians. The issue of "Cherokee Freedmen" is a hot debate. In the early 1980's the administration of the modern Cherokee Nation wanted to change this classification and revised their requirements saying that to belong to the Cherokee Nation required that an ancestor was *listed* as "Cherokee by Blood" on the Dawes Final Roll. On the Dawes Roll, the expression "Freedmen," designated that person was a former slave of the Five Tribes. According to the New York Times, March 3, 2007, *Putting to a Vote the Question Who Is Cherokee? by Evelyn Nieves,* "When the Dawes Rolls were created, those with any African blood were put on the Freedmen roll, even if they were half Cherokee. Those with mixed-white and Cherokee ancestry, even if they were seven-eighths white and one-eighth Cherokee, were put on the Cherokee by blood roll. More than 75 percent of those enrolled in the Cherokee Nation have less than one-quarter Cherokee blood, the vast majority of them of European ancestry."

To remove Cherokee Freedmen from the rolls would mean perhaps 25,000 Cherokees would no longer be considered Cherokee members. But in 2006, the Cherokee Supreme Court ruled that it was unconstitutional to keep these members out so they were re-admitted.

The Wallace Roll will give you a bit of information, similar to a census. A later roll called the *Kern-Clifton Roll* was done to gather the names Wallace missed. Search the Wallace Roll here: http://www.accessgenealogy.com/native/wallace-roll.htm

**Dawes List**: 1899 - 1907. The Dawe's List is still in use today by the *Five Tribes*. To gain membership in one of these tribes one must be descended from someone listed on the Dawe's List and be able to prove it. I've put the Dawe's List in a chapter all its own. See the next chapter *Searching the Dawe's Final Roll.*

**Guion-Miller Roll 1906 - 1909:** The Guion Miller Roll, also known as the Eastern Cherokee Emigrant Payroll was taken during the time period between August 1906 to May 1909. It's a list of Cherokee who filed for compensation after a US Claims Court ruling on May 28, 1906. One-hundred-thirty-three-dollars and thirty-three cents was allotted per person to those who had been relocated from the Southeast. Those Cherokees who had received earlier compensations in 1896 will not be found on the Guion Miller Roll. Furthermore, applications were separated between those who lived east of the Mississippi and those living west of the river. The Guion Miller Roll shows a lot of information including the Cherokee name along with the English name. Names of grandparents and brothers and sisters and both paternal and maternal information can be found, as applicants were encouraged to write down as much information as they could. If you find an application for *any* family members, don't just rely on the roll, study the application. The application of an uncle may have more names and information. Forty-six thousand people filled out applications. There is an online index through the National Archives. On the index you'll find both rejected and accepted application names. If you find an ancestor's name, you can contact the National Archives for a copy of the application. Some great instructions for searching this index can be found at this website:

www.tngenweb.org/cherokee_by_blood/miller.htm.

**1907 Census of Seminole County, Oklahoma** (on microfilm):
http://www.census.gov/history/www/genealogy/decennial_census_rec
ords/censuses_of_american_indians.html

**Baker Roll 1924 - 1931:** The Baker Roll, named after the man who completed it, Fred A. Baker, is also known as the *Final Roll of the Eastern Cherokee*. There is a later enumeration called the *Baker Revised Roll* and it is today's membership list for North Carolina Eastern Cherokee. Search the Baker Roll here:
http://www.accessgenealogy.com/native/1924-baker-roll.htm

**California Judgment Roll:**
An enrollment was taken of Indian children born since May 18, 1928. The enrollment was finalized in May 1933. In June of 1948 that enrollment was revised and approved on June 30, 1955. It included Indian children or their descendants, still living, that had been born as of May 18, 1928. This final roll has 36,094 names. It is called "The Revised Roll of California Indians" and can be obtained through the National Archives. Having an ancestor on The California Judgment Roll is sometimes a prerequisite for participating in beneficial programs.

There are other lists of names, censuses, payroll lists, even lists that show timber cutting permits. It becomes too complicated for me to include them. A good resource for information about the other lists is a pamphlet with the title, *Researching Individual Native Americans at the National Archives at Atlanta* you can read it online:

http://www.archives.gov/atlanta/finding-aids/Native-americans.pdf

*Access Genealogy* has other lists I have not mentioned. You can view them here: http://www.accessgenealogy.com/native/native-american-indian-rolls.htm

# Chapter Seven
## Searching the Dawes Final Roll

*Mrs. American Horse, Library of Congress*

When searching for Native American ancestry, you'll hear about the *Dawe's List*. It's another roll, list, enumeration, schedule, tally, etc. In 1893 a commission was assembled through U.S. Senator Dawes. This commission was created for the purpose of accepting applications from American Indians who **belonged to any one of the Five Civilized Tribes who resided in the Indian Territory**. The deal was, if the Indians abolished their tribal governments and accepted federal laws, they would receive a land allotment. The idea was to facilitate the assimilation of Natives into white culture and create the Cherokee nation that is now in Oklahoma. Because of their distrust of the government, many Natives did not come forward and apply. Because land was being allocated for Indians, and people can be greedy and deceptive, non-Indians filled out applications too. "The Final Rolls of the Citizens and Freedmen of the Five Civilized Tribes in Indian Territory," was what Dawe's enumeration was called. This tribal enrollment period would extend from 1899 to 1907. Of course, the list only includes those who chose to apply and were "approved" as belonging to one of these tribes: Cherokee, Chickasaw, Choctaw, Creek and Seminole.

If you are hoping to gain admission into the Cherokee tribe, you must find your ancestor's name on the Dawes Final Roll of 1907. **After** finding your ancestor on that roll, you'll want a copy of it for your records. Go to the National Archives Dawes Roll tutorial and follow their steps for obtaining a copy of your ancestor's Dawe's information. Remember, this is **AFTER** you confirm your ancestor is listed on the Dawes Final Roll of 1907.

http://www.archives.gov/genealogy/tutorial/dawes/

The correct way to research is to start with yourself and then to your parents and their parents, etc. while going through the records that you have, especially birth and death certificates. You'll need to prove that the name you find on the Dawes list is truly your relative. You must have the correct documents that make the connection from yourself to a parent and that parent to their parent. If you find your ancestor on the Dawes Final Roll of 1907, they will have a number associated with that name. This number is very important, if you are applying to become a Cherokee tribal member, it will go on your application. Native Americans who did not maintain connections to their tribes will NOT appear on these lists.

This list is the end of the road for those wishing to join one of the Five Civilized Tribes. In order to join, your ancestor's name must be on this final roll. It is used today to determine membership in the Cherokee Nation. To officially join the Cherokee tribe, the Dawes Final Roll is the last say.

The Oklahoma Historical Society has a website. There are two search bars on the page (see the link below). The first search bar will bring up a list of research and genealogical reference pages. Type in a surname and you'll see what research has been done on that name. Scrolling down to the second search bar will let you search the Dawes Final Rolls. http://www.okhistory.org/research/dawes.

You can also write to them:
Oklahoma Historical Society
Archives and Manuscripts Division
2100 N. Lincoln Blvd.
Oklahoma City, OK
73105
Phone #: 405-521-2491

Here is another link. This one is to the National Archives for Dawes list. Follow the directions carefully and be patient, it's interesting and may lead you to some truths.
http://www.archives.gov/research/Native-americans/dawes/intro.html

Dawes rolls are also available through:
Tulsa City-County Library
400 Civic Center
Tulsa, OK 74103
Phone #: 918-596-7977
website: www.tulsalibrary.org

or: www.tulsalibrary.org/collections/genealogy/roll-text.htm

Another interesting list of names and information is the rejected applications for the Dawes Roll. In 1896 Cherokee, Choctaw, Chickasaw and Creek Indians applied but were declined for one reason or another. The rejected applications contain historical records that have been saved over the years. These records also include evidence provided by applicants to prove that they should be considered for Indian citizenship. There are sometimes family member's names, marriage licenses and some photographs. Occasionally there is a family history. They were doing maintenance on the list while I was writing this book but here is the link:

http://www.accessgenealogy.com/Native/cherokees-choctaw-chickasaw-and-creek-1896-applications.htm

The Dawe's List is an enumeration taken of Indians that were *living in Indian Territory at the time the rolls were taken.* You may not know where they were living at the time, I certainly don't have all that information on my ancestors, I have too many to count, but many genealogists are armed and ready. They have census lists and know where their ancestors were between 1898 and 1906. Some of us just want to plug our ancestor's name in a search engine and voila! But it's not that easy. It is fun though, especially when you find the exact name of your ancestor, even though you know it's not them, it still gives you a lift. But it's not true and it's an identity that belongs to someone else. The Oklahoma Historical Society suggests you **look for your ancestor on the 1900 U.S. Census to see if they resided in Indian**

**Territory while people were being enrolled in the Dawe's List.** If not, they say it is "extremely unlikely" your ancestor will be on the rolls. And don't forget, many people were "rejected" from the Dawe's List, so there are rejected applications available to go through.

Now it's time to get your calculator out. If your ancestor is Fred Greene and you find a fellow by that name on the Dawe's List, you will need to match up the age of your ancestor with the age of the Fred Greene on the list.

Remember my timeline I displayed in *Chapter Two?* Because of my family oral history, I believe Martha V. Wright is a likely candidate to be of Native ancestry and sure enough, when I typed Martha Wright into the search field of the Dawe's List, a Martha Wright, **74-years-old** came up. Enrollment for the Dawe's List began in 1898 and ended in 1906. The date for the final roll was 1907. Most of the time, the ages on the rolls are the age the ancestor was about 1902. The Oklahoma Historical Society knows the lists well and has obviously matched enough birth certificates and other documents to confirm 1902 is usually the correct year to match the age.

1902 (approximate date for calculating the age your ancestor was when they enrolled)
-<u>1819</u> (birth year of my Martha Wright)
   **83** My Martha Wright's age in 1902.

Because this doesn't match with the *Final* Dawe's List, I would be foolish not to look at the *early* 1898 Dawe's List.

1898 (Ancestor could have enrolled this year)
-1819 (birth year of my Martha Wright)

**79** This is closer to the 74-year-old Martha Wright on the Dawe's Final List. If I can't match any other family names on the list of Wrights, I should probably give up on this ancestor and go on to another. This is the problem with not knowing which ancestor is the American Indian. Go back to your timeline and find another surname.

Any names on the Dawe's Roll listed as a **minor** or a **newborn** would have been born after 1898 and before March of 1907. These distinctions are also made:

**By blood** - Meaning your ancestor has a direct blood relation with the tribe or tribes

**Intermarriage** - Meaning that this ancestor was married to a tribe member

**Freedmen** - This was the term used for former slaves belonging to the tribes and the descendants of the slaves

**IW** - Intermarried White

When reading an Indian census, you may run across the expression "non-White" or in 1850 "Copper." You may also run across "In," for Indian, written in the column. In 1860 and 1870 the ethnicity will read "Indian." You may see an old census that says "colored" for the ethnicity of an ancestor but they could have been Native American, not necessarily African American.

Returning to my Martha Wright born in 1819 and listed as 74-years-old on the Dawe's List, it's a stretch but worth following up. She's listed as *full-blooded Chickasaw by blood*. But now what? I need to find her in a census record and see what ethnicity was submitted.

Even if this were not my Martha Wright, what we have confirmed is that a full-blooded Chickasaw woman could have a European name. Many but not all of the names on the Dawe's List are European-sounding names so it's a delight to run across authentic Native names. Depending on which website you're viewing the Dawe's List on, you might be able to click on the hyperlinked number next to their name and it will bring up other names, presumably family members or neighbors. If the names don't sound familiar don't rule it out... yet. Women are supposed to be listed under their married name but I'd try maiden names too.

For the sake of moving on, I've found a common name on my husband's family tree, Robert R. Taylor, born in 1895. I found a Robert Taylor on the final Dawe's list who is 7 years old.

 1902 (approximate date for calculating the age your ancestor was when they enrolled)

-1895 (Robert Taylor's birth year)

  **7**

Perfect age match except the Robert on the Dawe's List is a full-blooded "Choctaw by Blood," so I know they're not the same Robert Taylor, but let's pretend they are. The Dawe's List gives me his name, his sex, his percentile, his card number, the tribe and the roll number. You can contact the Oklahoma Historical Society at the link I provided. From them you may be able to order "enrollment packets" that provide further details about the person you found on the Dawe's List and their family. Don't forget, they had to be living in Indian Territory at the time the rolls were taken. That aspect is easy to forget.

Remember, census records will help you discover *where your ancestor lived* during the years the government made the tallies. If you are looking to gain enrollment in a recognized tribe, you'll need to find them *living in Indian Territory at the time the list was made*. When looking for free census records, I found this: http://www.censusfinder.com/. Scrolling down a little, on the left is a search box for states. Typing in the name of the state should bring up a variety of census dates. At some point Ancestry.com will ask that you create a free account. This is different than their free 14-day trial offer. A free account at Ancestry.com has allowed me to create family trees, search census records and collaborate with the genealogical community on the message boards.

You'll need to find the census records *after* the birth date of your ancestor. If they were born in 1876, look for the 1880 census. Going through census records is a tedious job. The originals are hard to read but a lot can be learned from them. You should study them for all the ancestors you have names and dates for. Having a name of a state your ancestor resided in is important and will make your search easier. If you only have an approximate birth year, the search engine will find the closest date to what you have. It will show you where your ancestor resided at the time of the census.

Suppose you get to the census and there is no mention of "Indian." Look at the other relatives and see if they've listed another ethnicity. If you're able to find parents, or grandparents, work backwards in time. Yes, it would be nice to find that your ancestors listed "Indian" but that may not be the case. Census records will tell you where your ancestor resided during those dates. Remember, to become an official tribal member your ancestor *must have been living in Indian Territory at the time the rolls were taken.* Remember the cession maps in Chapter Two? There are sixty-seven maps in all. These maps will help you get a feel for Indian territories. *US GenWeb Archives, United States Digital Map Library*: http://usgwarchives.net/maps/cessions/.

Operated by the United States Federal government, the National Archives job is to preserve and make federal records available to scholars and institutions. For instance, the Archives will sell you a copy of the Bill of Rights, they'll also sell you historic records the government kept on Indians but you'll have to buy them through their affiliate websites like ancestry.com. Native American gatekeepers use federal records to verify Indian ancestry for inclusion into their tribe. Here is the website for the National Archives:

http://www.archives.gov/research/Native-americans/

Here is their address:

National Archives & Records Administration

Southwest Region

P.O. Box 6216

Fort Worth, TX 76115

Email address: archives@ftworth.nara.gov

Of course, it's easy to type your surnames into the Dawe's search engine and see if anything comes up. Even though an ancestor wasn't living in Indian Country at the time Dawe's was taking his enumerations of Indians, I still might run the names. Scrolling through surnames is wise because you may have an ancestor named William who was listed as Willie. Being thorough is advised and it's easy to copy and paste names from the list. Say for example, there are 80 names under the Brewer surname. You can copy and paste them into a document on your computer and match them up later.

*Adoptions and Missions*

In the 1800's during times of Indian relocation, Indian children were put up for adoption. Tens of thousands of Indian children went through *The Carlisle school*. There was a study done on these schools and the study was such an embarrassment, President Hoover put money into improving the schools. Many adoptions occurred between 1825 and about 1850 and continued into the 1900's where children were taken from their homes, the claims of neglect unfounded.

Students at the Carlisle Indian School in Pennsylvania. Photo is housed at the Denver Public Library.

I wish I could say that the wrongs done to America's Native People have been rectified. But today, many people are still blind to the injustices that continue to be wrought on the people who were forced to leave their land and culture. I could write volumes about the poverty that many of our "First People" still endure. Lately, there have been many changes. Because of the sovereignty that many tribes have, they have entered into gambling and have become prosperous. They've built new communities and in Northern California where I live, there is a new American Indian medical center. They provide state of the art health care and have a dental clinic, an optometrist, gynecologist and a psychiatrist. All ethnicities are welcome but there is Indian preference for hiring and if one has proof that a Native American ancestor is "on the list," all the services are offered free of charge.

Involved in the health, social and educational welfare of their community, professionals of American Indian descent see to it that the needs and aspirations of Indian youth are met and keep pace with the changing times. In the Sierra Nevada mountain ranges, youth and cultural wellness programs offer American Indian children the skills they'll need to be self-sufficient and independent. There are education and career planning programs, teen pregnancy prevention programs, fatherhood programs, marriage counseling and workshops that provide the skills to maintain Native family values, including traditional marriage ceremonies. Here's hoping respect for Native American culture will grow exponentially and lead to health and prosperity for the coming centuries. If your Native ancestral trails are lost, I'm sorry. But as my Native American daughter-in-law always tells me, "We can build new trails."

# Dawe's List Worksheets

*Daughter of Chief Kamakur Nez Perce Tribe, Library of Congress*

I've provided a worksheet for calculating ancestors for the Dawe's Final Roll. You may have several ancestors you'd like to try. Enter your ancestor's birth date in the blank space and subtract it to come up with the age your ancestor was in 1902. This should match closely with the age of the name on the Dawe's Roll. Grab your calculator.

_____ Name

1902 (approximate date for calculating the age your ancestor was when they enrolled)

-____ (birth year of ancestor)

　　　Ancestor's age in 1902.

Notes:

_____ Name

1902 (approximate date for calculating the age your ancestor was when they enrolled)

-____ (birth year of ancestor)

     Ancestor's age in 1902.


Notes:


_____ Name

1902 (approximate date for calculating the age your ancestor was when they enrolled)

-____ (birth year of ancestor)

     Ancestor's age in 1902.

Notes:


_____ Name

1902 (approximate date for calculating the age your ancestor was when they enrolled)

-____ (birth year of ancestor)

Notes:

_____ Name

     Ancestor's age in 1902.

1902 (approximate date for calculating the age your ancestor was when they enrolled)

-____ (birth year of ancestor)

Notes:

_____ Name

     Ancestor's age in 1902.

1902 (approximate date for calculating the age your ancestor was when they enrolled)

-____ (birth year of ancestor)

     Ancestor's age in 1902.

Notes:

# *Interesting Websites*

*A Walker Lake Paviotso Indian, Library of Congress*

This website tells the history of the Indian census and has some great pictures and numerous links:

http://www.census.gov/history/www/genealogy/decennial_census_records/censuses_of_american_indians.html

This is an old census of tribes in the U.S. The history is particularly interesting and there are some hand drawn maps at the end:

http://www.census.gov/history/pdf/1890indiansreport.pdf

This is the National Archives website for thorough census information:

http://www.archives.gov/research/census/native-americans/1790-1930.html

In-depth website for Acadian history and genealogy. Many interesting links including one for Louisiana's German Coast history:

http://www.acadian-cajun.com/genacad1.htm

An interesting blog:

http://acanadianfamily.wordpress.com/2012/01/06/main-index-Native-american-names-of-quebec-and-ontario-marriage-documents/

This is a paper discussing Native American dental characteristics. I am no dentist so cannot confirm the scientific validity of this research. Toward the end the author mentions the words "thorny", and at other times makes it clear that some of this research is controversial. It is interesting though and shows diagrams of teeth:

http://www.uic.edu/classes/osci/osci590/10_1Non-Metric.htm

This website has a lot of thinking outside the box:

http://www.manataka.org/page2460.html

Very nice Lenape dictionary:

www.gilwell.com/lenape/lenape.pdf

Lots of complex Canadian Indian history from a journal written in the late 1700s. It's obviously written by a non-Indian and is biased but interesting:

http://www.archive.org/stream/journalofjlofque00lees/journalofjlofque00lees_djvu.txt

A comprehensive history of Native American history and culture, *Contributed by Sandra L. Cadwalader:*

http://autocww2.colorado.edu/~toldy2/E64ContentFiles/HistoryOfThe Americas/NativeAmericans.htm

This National Archives website has links to a few of the Indian rolls. It also has links to history and cultural information:
http://www.archives.gov/research/alic/reference/Native-americans.html

*Interesting book, it's a candid portrait of Indian life in Yosemite:*
IT WILL LIVE FOREVER, Traditional Yosemite Indian Acorn Preparation by Bev Ortiz, Heyday Books, Berkeley, Calif., 1991.

# *Bibliography*

http://www.accessgenealogy.com/

http://www.accessgenealogy.com/Native/tribes/abenaki/malecitehist.htm

The Atlas of the North American Indian, by Carl Waldman,
Checkmark Books, New York, NY, 2000.

Bureau of Indian Affairs

http://www.census.gov/history/www/genealogy/decennial_census_records/censuses_of_american_indians.html

http://autocww2.colorado.edu/~toldy2/E64ContentFiles/HistoryOfThe
Americas/NativeAmericans.htm, *Contributed by: Sandra L.
Cadwalader*

DEHUMANIZING NATIVE AMERICANS
http://www.worldfreeinternet.us/AmericanHolocaust/dehum.htm

DAUGHTERS OF THE EARTH, THE LIVES AND LEGENDS OF
AMERICAN INDIAN WOMEN, by Carolyn Niethammer,
Touchstone, Simon & Shuster, 1977, NY, NY.

Department of the Interior

ETHNOGENESIS OF THE METIS, CREE AND CHIPPEWA IN TWENTIETH CENTURY MONTANA, by J. Elizabeth Sperry B.A., Anthropology, University of Montana, Missoula, MT, 2001 B.A., Native American Studies, University of Montana, Missoula, MT, 2006.

First People of Tennessee and the American Southwest, by Fred Smoot    http://www.tngenweb.org/tnfirst/rolls.html

http://freepages.genealogy.rootsweb.ancestry.com/~richardrustybrewer/richardrustybrewerfamily.index.html

Grolier Encyclopedia, The Grolier Society Inc., 1956.

Health Characteristics of the American Indian and Alaska Native Adult Population: United States, 1999-2003, by Patricia M. Barnes, M.A.; Patricia F. Adams; and Eve Powell-Triner, Ph.D., U.S. Department of Health and Human Services, Centers for Disease Control and Prevention, Number 356, April 27, 2005.

HOW THERAPISTS FROM THE DOMINANT CULTURE CAN MOST EFFECTIVELY WORK WITH NATIVE AMERICAN CLIENTS, by Margo J. Hecker, The Graduate School University of Wisconsin-Stout, 2002.

Heart of Colonialism Bleeds Blood Quantum, Roy Cook http://www.americanindiansource.com/bloodquantum.html

http://imblackeagle.tripod.com/looks1.htm

The Low Dutch Company, A History of the Holland Dutch
Settlements of the Kentucky Frontier by Vincent Akers, 1982.

Native American Genealogy/Malecite History

New Advent, Catholic Encyclopedia
http://www.newadvent.org/cathen/07747a.htm

The Influence of Sephardic Jews and Moors on Southeastern Indian
Cultures, by Donald Panther-Yates
http://www.jewishindy.com/modules.php?name=News&file=article&s
id=8268

Putting to a Vote the Question 'Who Is Cherokee?' by Evelyn Nieves,
The New York Times (nytimes.com), March 3, 2007.

REPORT ON INDIANS TAXED AND INDIANS NOT TAXED IN
THE UNITED STATES (EXCEPT ALASKA), ELEVENTH
CENSUS 1890
http://www.census.gov/history/pdf/1890indiansreport.pdf

The Scribner-Bantam English Dictionary, Bantam Books, NY, NY,
1980.

THE UNDERGROUND RAILROAD, A RECORD OF FACTS, AUTHENTIC NARRATIVE, LETTERS, &C., Narrating the Hardships, by William Still, Porter & Coates, Philadelphia, Pennsylvania, 1872.

The USGenWeb Census Project, Cherokee, Native Americans of the Five Civilized Tribes (http://www.us-census.org)

www.ingramcontent.com/pod-product-compliance
Lightning Source LLC
Chambersburg PA
CBHW060152290526
45789CB00003B/1011